MW01165718

I Love My Pet

FROG

Aaron Carr

LET'S READ
AV²
BY WEIGL™
ADDED VALUE • AUDIO VISUAL

Go to www.av2books.com, and enter this book's unique code.

BOOK CODE

L 3 2 7 9 7 1

AV² by Weigl brings you media enhanced books that support active learning.

AV² provides enriched content that supplements and complements this book. Weigl's AV² books strive to create inspired learning and engage young minds in a total learning experience.

Your AV² Media Enhanced books come alive with...

Audio
Listen to sections of the book read aloud.

Key Words
Study vocabulary, and complete a matching word activity.

Video
Watch informative video clips.

Quizzes
Test your knowledge.

Embedded Weblinks
Gain additional information for research.

Slide Show
View images and captions, and prepare a presentation.

Try This!
Complete activities and hands-on experiments.

... and much, much more!

Published by AV² by Weigl
350 5th Avenue, 59th Floor New York, NY 10118
Website: www.av2books.com   www.weigl.com

Library of Congress Cataloguing in Publication data available upon request.
Fax 1-866-449-3445 for the attention of the Publishing Records department.

ISBN 978-1-62127-293-9 (hardcover)
ISBN 978-1-62127-299-1 (softcover)

Printed in the United States of America in North Mankato, Minnesota
1 2 3 4 5 6 7 8 9 0   16 15 14 13 12

122012
WEP301112

Project Coordinator: Aaron Carr   Art Director: Terry Paulhus

Weigl acknowledges Getty Images as the primary image supplier for this title.

2

I Love My Pet

FROG

CONTENTS

2 AV² Book Code

4 Frogs

6 Life Cycle

10 Features

14 Care

20 Health

22 Frog Facts

24 Key Words

24 www.av2books.com

3

I love my pet frog.
I take good care of him.

5

My pet frog was a tadpole.
He did not have any arms
or legs yet.

6

My pet frog
lived in water for 12 weeks.
He was full grown
after 16 weeks.

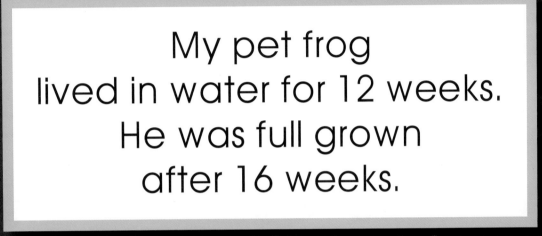

A young frog
that still has part of its
tadpole tail is called a froglet.

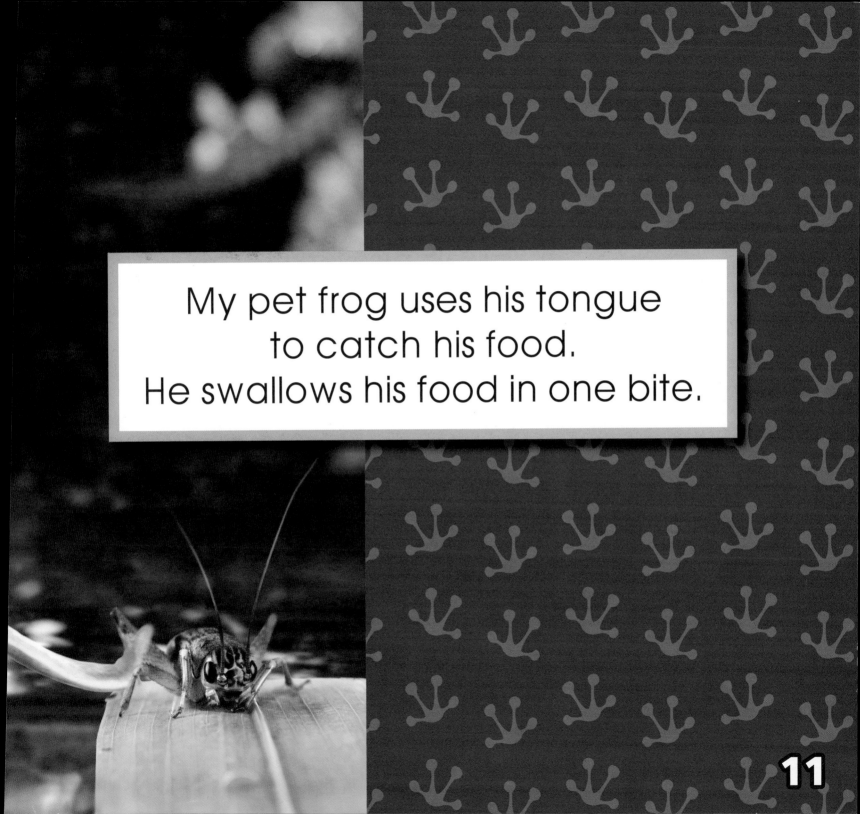

My pet frog uses his tongue
to catch his food.
He swallows his food in one bite.

My pet frog breathes through his skin. His skin also helps keep him safe.

A frog's skin is covered with poison.

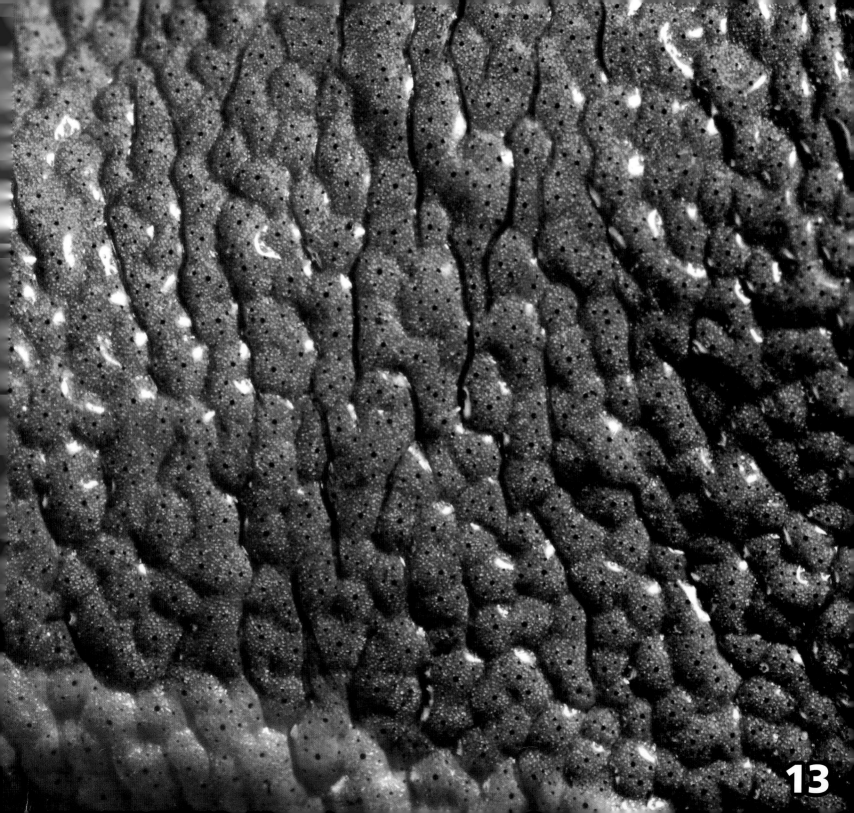

My pet frog is cold blooded.
He goes to sleep when he
gets too cold.

My pet frog
needs to be fed every day.
I have to clean his tank
every month.

My pet frog eats insects. He uses his large eyes to help him swallow his food.

Frogs drink water through their skin.

19

20

I help keep my pet frog healthy and happy.
I love my pet frog.

FROG FACTS

These pages provide more detail about the interesting facts found in the book. They are intended to be used by adults as a learning support to help young readers round out their knowledge of each animal featured in the *I Love My Pet* series.

Pages 4–5

I love my pet frog. I take good care of him. Frogs make great pets. Choosing the right frog is important. There are more than 4,000 frog species, but not all of them make good pets. First-time owners should start with a common frog, such as the green tree frog. This frog grows up to 4 inches (11 centimeters) long and lives up to 20 years.

Pages 6–7

My pet frog was a tadpole. He did not have any arms or legs yet. When frogs are born, they hatch from eggs. At this time, they are tadpoles. A tadpole does not look like a frog. It looks like a small fish, with a long, flat tail and a round mouth. Tadpoles stay underwater. They breathe through gills, like fish, and eat seaweed.

Pages 8–9

My pet frog lived in water for 12 weeks. He was full grown after 16 weeks. Four weeks after hatching, skin begins to grow over the tadpole's gills. By six to nine weeks of age, the tadpole starts to grow arms and legs. By 12 weeks, the tadpole has become a froglet. Froglets look like small frogs, but they still have a part of the tadpole tail. By 16 weeks, the frog's change, called metamorphosis, is complete.

Pages 10–11

My pet frog uses his tongue to catch his food. He swallows his food in one bite. The frog's tongue is sticky. The frog flicks its tongue out to catch its prey. Once the prey is stuck to the tongue, the frog pulls the food into its mouth. Frogs do not have teeth, so they must catch food that is small enough to swallow whole.

Pages 12–13

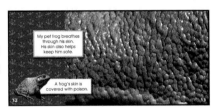

My pet frog breathes through his skin. His skin also keeps him safe. Frogs can absorb air through their skin. If they need more air, they can also breath through the nose. This causes the throat to bulge out as it fills with air. Frogs are covered in slimy mucus. The mucus is poisonous in all frogs, but it is not strong enough to affect humans in most species.

Pages 14–15

My pet frog is cold blooded. He goes to sleep when he gets too cold. Frogs are amphibians. Amphibian means "dual life," which refers to their early stages living in water and their adult life on land. Like all amphibians, frogs cannot make their own body heat. They need to be kept warm. If frogs get too cold, they will go into a deep sleep called hibernation.

Pages 16–17

My pet frog needs to be fed every day. I have to clean his tank every month. Compared to other pets, frogs do not need much care. They do not need to be walked, groomed, or cleaned. They need to be fed and provided with clean water every day, and their tank needs to be cleaned regularly.

Pages 18–19

My pet frog eats insects. He uses his large eyes to help him swallow his food. Animals that eat insects are insectivores. Frogs prefer to eat live insects, including crickets, grasshoppers, fruit flies, spiders, and earthworms. Frogs use their eyes to help swallow their food. They close their eyes and pull them inside the head. This pushes the food down the frog's throat.

Pages 20–21

I help keep my pet frog healthy and happy. I love my pet frog. Most frogs do not like to be handled, and some will bite if picked up. Small frogs could be hurt if picked up. Always get an adult's help when caring for your pet frog. If your pet frog stops eating, it might be a sign of illness. If your frog becomes sick, take it to a veterinarian for treatment right away.

KEY WORDS

Research has shown that as much as 65 percent of all written material published in English is made up of 300 words. These 300 words cannot be taught using pictures or learned by sounding them out. They must be recognized by sight. This book contains 51 common sight words to help young readers improve their reading fluency and comprehension. This book also teaches young readers several important content words, such as proper nouns. These words are paired with pictures to aid in learning and improve understanding.

Page	Sight Words First Appearance
4	good, him, I, my, of, take
6	a, any, did, have, he, not, or, was
9	after, called, for, grown, has, in, is, its, lived, part, still, that, water, young
11	food, his, one, to, uses
12	also, helps, keep, through, with
15	gets, goes, too, when
16	be, day, every, needs
19	eats, eyes, large, their
21	and

Page	Content Words First Appearance
4	care, frog, pet
6	arms, legs, tadpole
9	froglet, tail, weeks
11	bite, tongue
12	poison, safe, skin
15	cold
16	tank, month
19	insects
21	happy, healthy

Check out www.av2books.com for activities, videos, audio clips, and more!

1 Go to www.av2books.com.

2 Enter book code. L 3 2 7 9 7 1

3 Fuel your imagination online!

www.av2books.com